From My Heart To Yours

Katherine Cresswell

BookLeaf Publishing

India | USA | UK

Presentation by *BookLeaf Publishing*

Web: www.bookleafpub.com

E-mail: info@bookleafpub.com

ISBN: 9789358313642

First edition 2024

My Awakening - Finding my Mind!

People will tell you I've lost my mind
I'll tell you I've just found it!

I remember clearly every detail that let me here
(apart from the amazing insights I had during
my guided walk that night)

I believe they were just for me, my
remembering, to share in snippets when the time
is right.

I was enlightened, I saw the light, my many
meditations came to life!

Every cell in my body bursting to life, I could
really feel it, I was the light!

I got complete clarity on what I wanted, and
what is real.

My inner child was beginning to heal.

No more being told what to do.

Fed up of being the good girl, enough of you!

I sat in the darkness to see the light and the shooting star sent me right to my guide.

He knew I was coming, I was meant to be there.

We laughed and we joked, the genie was out.

We didn't really know what it was all about.

But on we went for a magical walk, where information was coming, I could decipher it all.

Every word had a meaning, every sound its own name, the universe was speaking, we were part of the game.

My mind was wide open so much info flowing in, it was just like 'The Secret' I'd found the key!!

Little did I know what was to come, all of the drama and then some!

No one understood, no one could see

The decisions I made were to set me free

Free from my life which was unfulfilling

Living with an addict, constantly downtrodden,
walking on eggshells, so much forgotten.

Breaking free from the past and the ancestry

Free from the worry and negativity

Its not been easy, it never will be

But I'm on my path and will always be me

Leaving You

Leaving you It's what I had to do,
I lived in hope for so many years
Fighting through all the tears
Trying to help however I could
 Doing what I thought I should
 Then one day I'd had enough
 I couldn't deal with all your stuff
I started working on myself
 Looking after my own health
That was the key
Refinding me and all the things I wanted to be
No more excuses, no more lies
I was discovering things deep inside
My purpose for being, my inner strength
Protecting my children and our future happiness
There had been too many chances wasted
Too many disappointments created
I finally realised I wasn't the one
I wasn't the one to deal with your problems
That was a job for you to do
Time for me to move on and find something new
Little did I know how much drama there would
be
Leaving you certainly hasn't been made easy
It makes me sad thinking what could have been

When we were all getting on, playing out the
happy family scene
There were just snippets, just fleeting moments
Covering up the hours of torment
I'm done with it now I can't hope any more
I'm just waiting for the day you walk out the
door
2 years it's been since I told you it's over
If only you were able to get sober

Taken

The moment I left you I said not to follow
But you couldn't just wait
Your mind is to hollow

All I wanted is for you to listen to a song
To listen to my meaning
What could go wrong?

I'd listened to you so many times
But you could keep your mouth shut no matter
how you tried

That was the tipping point,
That was enough
I had to get out and leave all my stuff

I collected our daugher she shouted at you
Even at 3 year old she knew what you should do
Go away Daddy, leave us alone
Why couldn't you have just stayed at home?

You told me that you'd tried to commit suicide
A broken glass left by your side
Why would I leave you with our kids
An alcholic depressive with so many needs

I thought I'd finally broke free but you still had
to come for me

Telling the police I'd lost my mind
The functioning alcoholic with white male
privileged on his side

I couldn't believe what then occurred
My beautiful children taken, how absurd!

No one would listen
No body cared

I stayed so calm and some how wasn't scared

I thought they were going to stay with a friend

If I'd know they were with you I'd have been
afraid

Then I was the one who was taken away

No handcuffs of sirens just a silent escape

Not able to go where I wanted to be
Unable to have my children with me

I got through it but knowing I was there to heal

Everything happening was so surreal

All the love, All the power as I stood at the door
Heart Fm on the tele and the police jacket I
wore!

Talking to people over & over again
Telling the story of what happened then

"I think its best that she stays for the night"

That suited me I didn't put up a fight!

Little did I know I was then led to a ward

No way out once they shut the door

They didn't tell me that I had been sectioned and
still there's no reason in my records

I was no harm to myself or anyone else

I was there to heal and discover myself

Appartently the problem was that I was elated

The doctor who told me that did get berated!

What is the problem with being happy

Oh well it might not last you see!

Yes I see doctor but thats part of life

Take the highs and the lows and deal with the
strife!

Such a challenging time but I go through it even
after all the bullshit that I had to deal with!

No Where to Go

What do you do when you've no where to go

Locked in a hell hole with people you don't know

What a crazy concept to help heal people with trauma

Take them away and take the drug order!

I refused all the drugs, I didn't need any

My Reiki and NLP skills gave me plenty

Plenty of strength to get through the days

Even after my escape plan dramatically failed

At least 5 people on top of me

Screens put around so others didn't see

They nearly broke my ankle and injected me

The poison from the apple into my butt cheek!

I shuffled around for the next few days

No medical checks, no sympathy!

They certainly made sure I wouldn't go far

No more running towards the door

My ankle was so swollen I could walk

Stuck on the ward but I didn't get bored

My own ensuite room and meals cooked for me

I had my radio and was able to sing!

The other patients were entertaining

There were times they needed healing

I even did healing for the staff

We did have some fun and time to laugh!

Thoughts

Thoughts are so powerful
Use them well
We are energetic beings
Full of cells
Fuel your body wisely and your soul too
You get one chance at this life and you get to
choose

There are laws in the universe
Universal truths
There's more than enough of everything
No one needs to lose

The Waves of Life

What you see is what you get
The truth, the light, what we so often forget
Lost in our lives and pleasing others, not
stepping back, hiding under the covers

All of the trauma we keep locked away
Stored as stress in our body, causing decay

From IBS to headaches and more
Each and every memory making you sore

Just pop a pill you'll soon feel better
Have an early night
Write someone a letter

Why not write a letter to yourself
Be kind, be true, let it all out
Get the feeling out any way that you can
Before they take over and bury you in sand

Every pain a little grain sliding through the timer
Life slipping away

Go to the beach, dip your feet in the sea, watch
the memories drift away

Breathe new life in

Do it now

Take a breath in through your nostrils, imagine
that sand

The sand that is drawn by the powerful water

Then breathe out through your mouth, breathe
away the trauma

Each wave a chance to renew and refresh

Washing away with every breath

A beautiful breath in tune with the sea

Curling your body and then releasing

Feeling the power

Hearing the sound

The sound of the waves coming in and hitting
the ground

Then slowly retreating and dragging the stones

The tiny fragments of ancient bones

Another reminder that we are basically clones!

All linked together through ancestral lines

Made of star dust from the start of time

All part of the story, part of you and me

Tiny particles bought together to make new
history

What a wonderful way to spread love from
above

Across the waves and across the world

Curing the ocean, curing the globe

Praise everything, every beauty filled drop

Fill yourself up till you're ready to pop

When your cup is full then you can help others

The circle of life, giving like mothers

The more that you give, the more that you gain

Then you can give again and again

No Limits

There are no limits to what you can do

No threshold set on what you can use

Gratitude
Kindess
A smile or a kiss

Sharing a compliment

It really is bliss

The ripple effect of the good vibrations, they
carry so far, across all nations.

You have the power to change the world

One smile at a time, one kind word

We can all come together and learn to exist in a
glorious state of utter bliss!

No Fear

No more bullshit
No ore fear
Switch of the TV
Don't drink all the beer
Find your true being
Don't mask the pain
There's nothing to loose
There's so much to gain

Revelations

The messages began firing again
I was clearing my body and my soul
This was it
Completely letting go

I was talking so quickly
Making so many connections

So much made sense
It was so intense

Coming to my senses
It was exactly that

Bodily fluids flowing
I had no control, it was pouring out
Cleansing my body inside and throughout
Washing away the years of pain
The pent up frustration
Pouring down like rain

The hospital treatment my mum received
My miserable midwife who made me want to
leave

My ex now being there when my daughter was
born

This was my rebirth
My chance to retell it all

Sobbing so hard
Then smiling with glee

Is this really happening to ME??

I was so aware of all that was happening
Man U playing football, my brother waiting for
them to score

That's it! I cried

Man United what we should all stand for

Coming together
Complete harmony

No need for hatred
No need for tyranny

I realised again its all within me
There is no one else

I am free

But my freedom was taken in physical form
My physical body was confined within 4 walls

My spirit was one thing that they couldn't touch
I had so much strength and used it so much

My faith and my trust got me through
Now I am able to share it with you

Going in!

A whole new challenge
A whole new way to be
Walking into the mental health facility

Just me in a robe and my dress on me

My brother decided to take my phone
Being protective so I'd be left alone

This was it.
I have nothing at all.

Just the clothes on my back and the will to go on

I knew it was my calling

I came here for healing

Not just myself but all under this ceiling

I had to go through the initial checks

A beautiful lady who was very calm

She respected my wishes

No blood from my arm

No covid test either

No other invasive procedures

Blood pressure, weight, height and pulse

Why is that important? All for the drugs!

What shall we give if blood pressure too high?

What if she's fat? This pill might make her die!

Why not sit and talk about feelings

Not just stare at a chart to see what it is
revealing

After this its a bit of a blur

A beautiful bearded lady I did observe

We had a connection straight away

She helped save me that fateful day

Calling me my mother in laws name!

Helping heal trauma from her family ways

The generations of worry, of guilt, of fear and shame

All the things I don't want my children to gain

All this time to spend with my thoughts

Writing is therapy, more needs to be taught

Artwork too so good for you

Letting things out, being free, attuned.

Tune into your feelings and let them flow

Its so much better when you let them go

Feeling low

When you reach a new low there's more room to
grow

Making room for the power within to help you
start again and begin

Begin to build the life you want

Letting go of all the strife

Getting the things you want in your life

The phoenix from the flames

Leave behind a blazing trail

Burning what's left and setting sail

Going with the flow, where you always know

You will end up where you're meant to be

You need to trust and keep the faith

You don't need to be caught in anyone else's race.

Make your own path, follow your heart

Life is a movie, play your part

You are the star of your show

Life it the best you can, show everyone what you know

Another Challenge

Another day filled with another challenge
I didn't get a chance to write

I was in the midst of my healthcare fight

Trying to get the doctor to see
This is the 'normalist' version of me!

I'm happy, I'm joyful, I love to dance

Sorry if that doesn't fit your stance

Scrutinising my every move

Always having something to prove

Acting 'normal' with nothing to loose

Freedom gone, away from my kids

Relying on others to get me out of this mess

Chastised for my beliefs, basically told to get a
grip

My grand ideas of a healing centre

I have it planned, its going to happen

My messages of positivity

Do they really help? They questioned me

I offered to show them the messages I had

Of all the people who enjoyed my posts

Now I am not usually one to boast

But my messages of positivity make a
difference, not just for me

The doctors didn't see that, they didn't want to
believe that a few words a day could give people
relief

If only they could get their heads from their
books and actually take a holistic look

Stop just filling people with drugs

They are humans with traumas, not just tummy
bugs!

Free Will

Another request. Another 2 hours

No water in here

What does that matter?

I'm only human with a vicious disease

One that apparently brings people to their knees!

Well I'm fit and healthy and know what I need

Perhaps if more people were they wouldn't be
afraid when they sneezed!

Cover up the pain my dear

Pop another pill

No thanks you greedy pharma c*nts

I'd rather use free will

My free will to think and ponder

What's happening with my body it's really a
wonder

Why is so much info misused?

No wonder most people are so confused!

Have you read the side effects on the label

Do you really think those tablets will make you
more stable?

Why not get to the underlying cause?

Sort out the problem

Don't just ignore

No wonder the world is full of depression,
alcoholic dependants and whatever suppressants.

Carrying around so much trauma.

Don't you know it's passed onto your sons and
daughters?

Open your hearts and open your minds

Your bodies are amazing

You'd be surprised!

Yes even yours, you can do it

Just take the leap and trust a bit

Step by step, day by day

You'll find an even healthier way

More ways to smile

More ways to have fun

A sense of freedom

A new life begun!

So empty your cupboards

Get rid of the crap

Come and see me, let's have a chat

I've plenty to tell you about the things that I've done

I'm proof that it works

Yes I am, No 1!!

Frustration!

This is such bullshit!
I can't take much more
A whole corridor in lockdown
They're winning the war!

Yes I've got covid
I'm stuck in my room
I've hardly fucking noticed
No symptoms at all

All it is is a glorified cold
Yes it can be complicated
It can be cruel
It was designed that way in the labs of Whutan

The powers that be rubbing their hands in glee
This time they've done it
They've put us under
Total control
Watch as they crumble

The whole fucking ward on a 10 day lockdown

You're having a laugh, dressed up like clowns!

Don't make out you're protecting our interests

You're lining your pockets and being greedy pricks!

Oh what irony, what fuckwittery

People let out for their cigarette fix

That's it darling add that to the mix!

Nicotine and tar to clog up your lungs
Your vape? Ok! In it goes!

More toxins, more poisons, coursing through your veins

Tell me why you're not feeling well again?!

Seriously people, time to wake up!

Take some responsibility, don't be a sup

It's so hard talking to a brick wall

The years of cnditioning making you conform

It's not your fault its how they want you to be

Zombified, programmed, just follow me!

The adverts will tell you what you need

Every post on your news feed

Then they'll blame you for feeling shitty

Putting pressure on the NHS, such a pity!

When will you realise they really don't care

The big corporations want to keep you there

Pumping you full of their profit fuelled drugs

Keeping you addicted, they really are thugs!

Incompetence

Fuck me! Come on
Yet another example
What a disaster
You reach out to speak to someone to help
Sorry darling, wrong number
Have you a pen?
The numbers on the leaflets are wrong
Just another test, something stay strong
You've got the number now
But no fucking answer
I'll say it again
This place is a disaster!

Looking back

We both know it had been building for so long
Living our own lives, bumbling along

Not really connecting just co-existing
Having huge arguments in the kitchen

I had to walk away, we both know why
I'd given so much, I had nothing left to try

I thought that you got it when we sat on the sofa
I just wanted you to listen, just for a few minutes
But that was too much, that's what finally did it!

The song words were saying so much to me
As clear as day, saying what I believed

I really, really wanted to stay but your love was
the illusion, I had to walk away

Protecting the children from all that I know

So they wouldn't inherit such fears and beliefs

Avoiding countless years of grief

After all of the work on my healing
I realised that so many things needed releasing

The grief of losing my dear mum

The traumatic birth

Never feeling like I was put first

Not really listened to

Told what to do

Enough of that everyone! Fuck you!

Open your minds

I'm not a little girl any more

I'm a fully grown woman

I don't want to be ignored

I've learnt so much and I want to share it

You've got an argument, ok, let's compare it

Bring your facts to me but do me a favour, take mine in too, don't just dismiss them because you don't know

I've done my research, I'm in charge of my show!

Not blindly following what we are told

That's not for me, time to be bold.

To finally stand up for what I believe in

Accepting no less, keeping dreaming

All the affirmations and positive thinking

Manifesting miracles, everything linking

I'm so bloody glad I've stood by my beliefs

They've seen me through this week full of grief

I'm clever, connected, I know my own body

I would love to help others cut crap from their diet

Putting in the good stuff, avoiding the ongoing riot

The bombardment of sugar and synthetic produce, all designed to make you feel useless!

The filling your minds with such utter crap

Rip up their rule book, create your own map!

All of your cells processing poison

Making you bloated, giving skin disorders

It's not just your food it's beauty products too

Everything you put on you

bsorbed by the skin, the biggest organ

Causing cancers and attacknig like a trojan

Now for one of the biggest pollutants

The media machine that's here to control us

You may call it a conspiracy

Just do your research then come back to me

It's never sat right these big corporations

Controlling our screens and controlling our
nations

They are in it together, the supreme elite

With their own agendas, keeping their lives
sweet

What tortured souls they must have

Knowing what they do

It fills me disgust

I've been down the rabbit holes

Seen the lies

The glitterati flashing them before our eyes

Just open your minds a little bit ore

Let some new information through your door

My Mission

Life was much simpler before my journey began

But that wasn't for me

That wasn't the plan

A path to enlightenment when I was ready

It came pretty quick

Quite unexpected

I still can't believe what I've been through

That fateful night walking under the moon

So much information coming through

Things making sense

Everything brand new

It was like something you see in a film

Some deluded genius breaking the codes

Its happened to others, it happened to me

I do understand it can seem frightening

Completely wired, like sky high on drugs

But this was all natural, the best kind of buzz!

They call it ascending, seeing the light

That is exactly what happened that night!

I'm here for a reason, part of a mission

The help heal and comfort

All part of my vision

It really is true, you can have all your want

Now its time for dreams to be built

Dream time

Still no pyjamas but time to sleep.
Hopefully for the last time in my temp home for
the week.
I've made it quite cosy. Tidier than home.
Getting room service and plenty of time on my
phone!
It won't get the best Trip advisor rating.
Some of staff need seriously berating!
But as I go to sleep tonight in my sterilised bed.
I'll be going to the sweetest places in my head.
Flying over all those that I love Sprinkling
happiness and peace from above.
Each night I take a different route. Crossing the
river, seeing my boat.
Flying over Jimmy's Farm. Sweet memories of
having my children in my arms. Tonight I think
I'll go to the beach Felixstowe is calling It's easy
to reach.
Just up the A14 I shall go
To see the waterfront and twinkling lights glow
The sound of the waves and the kids having fun
Splashing in the sea and going for a run
Eating fish and chips out of paper bags
Seagulls stealing chips, chasing dad!

I'll have a whole new appreciation for these
simple things
For being able to stand out in the breeze.
Free to be me Without being judged
Free to spread happiness, joy and love. T
hat's all that I want. That's who I am.
Unfortunately most people here don't understand
But no one and nothing will dampen my spirit
I've been to hell and back and I'm still here with
it
Soon I'll be back where I belong
This time making sure no more can go wrong

My Fate

So tomorrow I face my biggest test ever
So please everyone pray together
1130am I have my meeting
Where complete strangers decide if they can
release me
It's really been something, it's opened my eyes
I'm surprised I've got any more tears to cry
But please don't feel sorry or worried or sad
The lesson is this, trust in all that you have
The power within you, the strength of your mind
Stay true to your values and you can decide
What's going to happen What your fate will be
You can make your mark in history.
This is the start of me making mine.
A future so wonderful It's going to be devine!
I've earnt it, I'm worthy of all that and more
I'm welcoming everything good to my door
No more drama, no more excuses
This is the life and this is how I choose it!
Just as I finished writing this verse I heard the
cheers from Portman Road
Come on you Blues Let's have a winner
Now get me back home in time for my dinner!

A Home Full of Love!

My heart is bursting.... I saw my babies tonight!
They're doing so well.
I want to hold them so tight!
Being with them, making them laugh, telling
them they need to have a bath!
They are just so beautiful, really a dream.
So lucky to have them, so blessed, so serene.
Not long now, mummy will soon be home.
Just for now we'll rely on the phone.
I've sent you some reiki and see you in my
dreams.
You know when I see you I'll give you the
biggest squeeze.
A shower to kisses, I don't know if I'll stop.
My heart will be filled up, right to the top.
You are oh so loved and oh so precious.
The most valuable treasure we could ever
possess.
More wanted than diamonds and gold, I want
nothing less, than you to be happy, your hearts to
be full, to take away any sadness.
This is just part of our amazing story.
Paving the way for so much glory.

There's never anything I've wanted more than to
see your beautiful faces when I walk through the
door.
It won't be long now, I promise you that.
I'm doing all that I can, wearing whatever hat.
The doctors will tick all the right boxes and set
me free, there are always choices.
With everything I have been through this week.
My human strength has shone through.
I've shown I'm not weak.
It seems I can handle most things.
But no more challenges, just get me home please